Hope for a
Mom's Heart

Hope for a Mom's Heart

*Help & Healing For Those Grieving
Pregnancy Loss Or Early Childhood Death*

MERRI ELLEN WRIGHT

TATE PUBLISHING
AND ENTERPRISES, LLC

Published by Tate Publishing & Enterprises, LLC
127 E. Trade Center Terrace | Mustang, Oklahoma 73064 USA
1.888.361.9473 | www.tatepublishing.com

Tate Publishing is committed to excellence in the publishing industry. The company reflects the philosophy established by the founders, based on Psalm 68:11,
"The Lord gave the word and great was the company of those who published it."

Book design copyright © 2014 by Tate Publishing, LLC. All rights reserved.
Cover design by Rodrigo Adolfo
Interior design by Jake Muelle

Published in the United States of America

ISBN: 978-1-62563-835-9
1. Religion / Christian Life / Death, Grief, Bereavement
2. Family & Relationships / Parenting / Motherhood
13.12.20

Dedicated
in Loving Memory to:

Gary Wayne Wright 2-16-71 to 4-28-73

(my husband's little brother)

Baby Wright 10-02-92

Baby Wright 11-10-95

Baby Wright 4-16-97

and to:

Your Baby or Child

Special Acknowledgements

A special note must be included to everyone at Iron Sharpeneth Iron, a ministry of Ironwood in Newberry Springs, California, who originally made this book a reality. To those who first saw the potential in my manuscript and to "the team" who walked through the nitty-gritty details of getting *Hope for a Mom's Heart* into print, I say thank you. Without your extraordinary encouragement and facilitation, *Hope* would not be in the hands of Tate Publishing now.

To my dear friend and original editor, Beneth Perry, I must offer my deepest appreciation. Her patience and guidance, wonderful suggestions, and liaison efforts could never be taken for granted. Without Beneth, my fumbling words would still be fumbling. I am indeed blessed by the friendship we formed over this project.

Thank you from the bottom of my heart to my parents, Jim and Regina Howard, and to the many supportive family members and friends who prayerfully uplifted me at the times when I needed it most. My dad had more influence than he will ever know on my manuscript finally being published.

I would be amiss not to express my gratitude to the special ladies who shared their stories of loss so that others could see how God's guiding hand worked in their lives. It is no easy task to revisit the pain of the past and then divulge those memories for the benefit of others.

I must also thank my Lord for giving me my wonderful husband, Greg, who was at my side through each difficult loss. Greg has not only been an emotional pillar for me but also has been my spiritual leader who always points me to the truth that God is good and only wants the best for us. I love you, Hon.

And finally, to all those who encouraged me along the way, I say, like the Apostle Paul, "I thank my God upon every remembrance of you" (Philippians 1:3).

Table of Contents

Letter of Introduction

*M*y Dear Friend,
  Having gone through three miscarriages, I can truly say that it does not matter how far along a woman is in her pregnancy when a miscarriage happens, the loss is still very real and can be devastating for both mothers and fathers. Mothers, especially, can be left feeling empty—both physically and emotionally—and hopeless, helpless, and hurt.

Here at the very beginning of this book, I want you, dear Mom, to know that Jesus Christ, who is God, stands waiting to offer you hope, help, and healing through his precious Word, the Bible. My desire is not just to share my personal experiences in such a way that you will be able to relate and say, "Oh, she does understand," but rather to help you see my great God who brought me through three miscarriages and truly brought the hope, help, and healing that I needed and that you may be seeking, as well.

I would like to start by introducing you to Jesus Christ and by explaining to you why he is the one to whom you need to turn right now. Jesus Christ came to the earth with one purpose in mind—to take on himself the punishment of every person's sin so that all of mankind could spend eternity with him in Heaven forever. Romans 6:23 tells us that the payment for sin is death, and Jesus paid the price of sin by his death on the cross. He then went on to conquer death by his burial and resurrection. Now, he offers to any who will take it, this gift of eternal life that he purchased. You may accept his gift by acknowledging that you are a sinner, and therefore deserve to be separated from God for eternity, and by believing in faith that his payment for your sins is sufficient for your salvation. You receive his salvation by simply talking to him through a prayer such as this:

> Dear God, I know that I am a sinner, and I understand that my sin will separate me from you for all of eternity. I am asking for your forgiveness of my sins, and I am accepting your death on the cross, your burial, and your resurrection as the payment that purchased a place in heaven for me. Thank you for this wonderful gift of salvation. Amen.

Salvation is really the first step you must take to have true hope, help, and healing. If you have already accepted Christ's gift of salvation, let me encourage you to review the message of God's saving grace. Nothing and no one else will be able to sustain you during this trial as Christ can.

My first miscarriage occurred at eight weeks gestation, and my third miscarriage happened at ten weeks. Both fit a similar pattern that I now understand to be the normal routine at the onset of a threatened miscarriage. I had to go through agonizing days of waiting to see what was going to happen and endure blood tests and ultrasounds to determine if the pregnancies were progressing. When the doctors determined that the babies had in fact died, they performed a dilation and curettage, also known as a D&C, to terminate each pregnancy. In both cases, the doctors told me that something had probably been wrong genetically with my babies.

My second miscarriage, however, was much different from my first and third. It occurred in that rather gray period between being termed a miscarriage and being termed a stillbirth. Either way, it had been a normal pregnancy up until my twenty-week ultrasound, during which the technician asked me some odd questions, giving me a very uneasy feeling. I tried asking him questions, but he quickly told me that he could not disclose anything and that I would have to wait for my doctor to speak with me. I left there on that Friday feeling like something was terribly wrong but unable to get any information—not even the gender of my baby, because the technician could not determine it. I believe this was the beginning of the Lord preparing me for the awful events of the next week. A guest speaker at our church, having no knowledge of the unrest in my heart, brought a message on Sunday that left me in a lake of tears, because I was realizing and accepting that God was indeed preparing me for a very difficult trial.

My doctor's appointment several days later started with a review of the ultrasound. Everything looked fine. What a relief to my silly, fearful heart—reading into everything like that! Then the but came—but the baby was measuring small for the due date. The doctor suddenly declared the due date to be wrong. I remember trying to compute the ultrasound's fifteen weeks gestational measurements versus the twenty weeks I knew to be correct. Something was wrong, and it was not my due date. Then, to move on and allay my worries, the doctor said, "Well, let's listen to the heartbeat." Gladly! He got a fetal heart monitor, and we both began listening with much anticipation. He moved it all over for what felt like an eternity and then finally, with a concerned look on his face, said something to the nurse about getting a different monitor. She came back shortly with another device, and still he could not find the heartbeat. By this time, my heart was broken because I knew he was desperately trying to prove my child was still alive. Of course, I had to go through another ultrasound to confirm our loss and then through several more grueling hours to determine the best course of action. The next day my pregnancy abruptly ended. I felt as if I were living in a nightmare; but at the same time, I was fully aware that this was not something I would merely awake from and find all to be well.

We had to wait many weeks for the autopsy report to come back, but at least we did get an answer for our baby's death. The umbilical cord had a knot in it, pulled so tightly that the doctor did not even see it, accounting for the small size of the baby. For weeks, vital nutrition had not been getting through, thus stunting growth and development and ultimately leading to death.

I do not know why God took my babies, but I do know that instead of experiencing hopeless despair during those three difficult times, I found hope in his love and comfort through a peace that I would have never experienced otherwise. The help that I found in his Word and claimed for my own was the healing balm that both my soul and body needed.

No matter how you may have come to possess *Hope for a Mom's Heart*, you probably have one main reason for beginning to read it; you are looking for hope and want answers that will help the hurt and calm your troubled heart right now. But hope is an expectation of something beneficial in the future. Your natural tendency will be to quickly read the pull-out quotes and the Additional Helps, trying to take a short cut to find that hope. Instead, will you accept my challenge to read the entire book as it is laid out and then use the Additional Helps as tools to reference when needed later? Lasting hope will not be found in a condensed, rushed version but rather in the thoughtful application over time of the principles found in each chapter.

Does my heart still ache at times for my babies that I never had a chance to hold? Yes. I am fully convinced that will always be a part of my life. However, I no longer feel hopeless, helpless, or hurt, because through Christ I have the assurance that I will one day get to meet my other three children and with them worship for eternity the One who planned our lives from beginning to end.

Because of His Hope,
Merri Ellen

If the Lord had not been my help, my soul would soon have lived in the land of silence. When I thought, "My foot slips," your steadfast love, O Lord, held me up. When the cares of my heart are many, your consolations cheer my soul.

Psalm 94:17-19 ESV

Grief — Yours and Others

he Sunday following the loss of one of our babies, my husband preached a message concerning David and how he dealt with the loss of his child. During the whole sermon, my heart kept crying out, "But what about Bathsheba?" During the days that followed, I could not get that question out of my mind. How did she deal with the loss of her baby? The Bible says very little about Bathsheba following the baby's death. However, the Bible does say in II Samuel 12:24 that David comforted her, providing a safe assumption for us that she grieved the loss of her baby.

A brief overview of the story of David and Bathsheba will ensure that we are on the same page and help you see that, while I am not condoning the sin by which their baby was conceived, I do believe that there are valuable lessons and applications that we can make concerning the loss of a child.

Second Samuel chapter 11 introduces us to Bathsheba, who was not supposed to be David's wife at all. Her husband was Uriah, the Hittite, as the Bible refers to him. He was a noble soldier in King David's army and was at war for his king. The Bible tells us nothing of Bathsheba's intentions when she bathed on her rooftop, but King David saw her and had her brought to his castle, and their relationship produced a child. To try to cover his sin, David then brought Uriah home from battle expecting him to go home to Bathsheba and enjoy her as his wife. However,

Uriah refused to allow himself such pleasantries while his comrades were sleeping in fields and at war. His nobility cost him his life, because David sent instructions to Uriah's captain to put him in a place of battle where Uriah was sure to become a casualty of war. Following the mourning period for her husband, David took Bathsheba and married her. Not allowing David to hide his sin so easily, God sent his prophet Nathan to confront him and declare God's judgment on him for the sins of adultery and murder. The penalty was the death of their baby.

In a very short amount of time, Bathsheba took on many different roles—David's lover, Uriah's widow, David's wife, and last, a grieving mom. My purpose is not to speculate exactly how Bathsheba dealt with her loss, but rather to share from my heart how in thinking about her situation, I, with help and counseling from my husband, came to some biblical conclusions concerning my losses that ultimately led me to a better understanding and acceptance of God's decision for my life. Thus began my journey toward healing; may it also be the beginning for you.

A Mother's Grief

About a week after losing our second baby, a Christian neighbor came over for a visit just to encourage me a little bit. Whether she intended to or not, she began my healing process. What earthshaking thing did she do? She simply asked what had happened and then patiently listened as I told her the details of our loss, beginning from a week before I lost the baby when the routine ultrasound indicated that other than the baby being small, everything was fine, to the horrifying moment of the doctor's not finding a heartbeat, all the way through the next few days that seemed like an eternity. She did not give advice or even say she understood; she just listened. For me, the first step in the healing process was to talk to a friend about what happened; and I would encourage you also to find someone you feel comfortable talking to. Recounting the details will be painful, but it will help you put things into perspective a little better and help you begin accepting what has happened.

In addition to talking to someone outside the family, you must talk to your husband. While his grief is different from yours (to the point that you may even wonder if the loss has fazed him at all), be assured that he, too, is grieving. As one, the two of you must work through this life-changing event; and in so doing, you will emerge with a renewed and strengthened relationship. So, if you feel you cannot talk to anyone else right now, sit down with your husband and a box of tissues and just talk. Hearing his perspective will help you realize that you are not as alone as you may have thought. Quite possibly, you may bring comfort to him as well by this joining together of grief.

While talking to a friend and your spouse can help in the healing process, the One who can help more than anyone else is the Lord; and it is he to whom you must never quit talking. Immediately following a tragedy such as a loss of a child, the Lord may seem very distant. I had trouble praying, even though I was not angry at God or blaming him. I believe this is a time when the Holy Spirit intercedes on our behalf and comforts us through this deep sorrow. Romans 8:26 says, "Likewise the Spirit also helps in our weaknesses. For we do not know what we should pray for as we ought, but the Spirit Himself makes intercession for us with groanings which cannot be uttered." After losing our first baby, I really thought that if I ever had to go through something like that again, I would lose my mind, as well. During our second loss, which was much more difficult for me, I was and still am amazed at the peace that the Holy Spirit gave me over and over again. My whole world seemed out of control, and yet there was a calmness that was not of my own volition. Isaiah 26:3 became very real as I truly was in perfect peace during that difficult journey. As you cry out to God letting his spirit and word be a healing balm for your aching heart, you too will experience "the peace of God, which surpasses all understanding" just as I did in the trial of our third miscarriage.

As you deal with your grief, remember two things—don't blame God and do trust God. While you may never understand your loss, God has brought it about for a reason; and blaming him will only hurt you. He sovereignly directs each of our lives and knows what is best for us. Blaming

God will break your fellowship with him at a crucial time when you need his help and guidance and will prevent you from tapping into his ever-present reservoir of love and comfort.

Trusting God is not as easy as it may sound. It is one thing to say, "I don't blame God"; but it is still another thing to come before His throne saying, "Your way is best for me." Matthew J. Slick of Christian Apologetics and Research Ministry shares the following regarding God's sovereign plan for his family.

> A few years ago, my wife and I were expecting our second child. At six months, after one of the routine exams during pregnancy, the doctor discovered a problem with the baby. Our child, whom we named Jacob, had holoprocencephaly—a chromosome problem that resulted in various deformities in Jacob's body. In short, Jacob could survive in the womb, but would most certainly not be able to survive outside it. Our son was going to die. We prayed and asked the Lord to miraculously heal Jacob during the remaining three months of pregnancy. We prayed and trusted God. Finally, when it was time for Jacob to be born, my wife endured the pains of childbirth and delivered Jacob into our hands. One half hour later, the Lord took him home. Jacob died in our arms.
>
> After the funeral and after many tears, people came up to us and wanted to know how we were

doing. We told them that in spite of the pain and the loss, we were fine. We had trusted God and relied on His wisdom, not ours, to handle the situation. We knew that because God was sovereign, that He had allowed us to suffer this trauma. And, even though we did not understand why, my wife and I were able to trust God to know that HE understood why. We would simply find out when we finally went to be with the Lord ourselves.[1]

Mr. Slick goes on to say that he learned through this trial that when we suffer great loss, we must believe that God still loves us; and we must trust Him beyond our ability to comprehend.

Two verses that have given me great peace, comfort, and trust in God's will have been Isaiah 55:8-9: "'For My thoughts are not your thoughts, Nor are your ways My ways,' says the Lord. 'For as the heavens are higher than the earth, So are My ways higher than your ways, And My thoughts than your thoughts.'"

A Father's Grief

While fathers can deal with their grief using the same principles that mothers use, fathers will grieve much differently from mothers. Many fathers never really develop that deep bond that mothers experience because of the physical changes of pregnancy; therefore, a miscarriage may not have as great an impact on them as on the mothers.

However, others may feel the loss quite keenly, especially if the death is not a miscarriage. Often, fathers take a back row seat to their wives, who more naturally grieve openly and therefore are the main ones to receive comfort and encouragement from friends and family. Some fathers readily accept the sovereign will of God and then quickly jump back into life. Though loving and supportive, Greg, fit into this category. He grieved, but nothing like I did. I believe we find a similar example illustrated in the lives of David and Bathsheba.

Prior to his child's death, David begged God for his baby's life. In II Samuel 12:16-17, we see David refusing to eat and lying on his face day and night before God. He fasted and prayed until the child died the seventh day; but in verse 20, after David learned of the child's death, he got up, washed himself, went to worship the Lord, and then ate. These actions may seem a bit bizarre for a father who has just lost a child, but David explained himself in verses 22 and 23. Because he knew there was hope for his son while the child was still alive, David begged God to spare him; but after the Lord took the child, there was no longer any reason to fast and pray. God had answered his prayer, even though the answer was not as he desired; and the correct response for him now was to accept God's answer and go on. This response included cleaning up, worshipping God, eating, and then returning home to comfort his family, especially Bathsheba. David's lack of outward grief seems to have made even the servants question his mental stability, yet David assured them that his mourning was while the child was still alive. While David was able to quickly move on after the death of the child, verse 24 of II Samuel 12 indicates that Bathsheba was still grieving, because the Bible tells us there that David comforted her. This is a great example of how men and woman deal with the loss of a child differently.

A Family's Grief

As private and personal as this loss is, it must be shared, nonetheless, with other members of the family, both immediate and extended. Children in the family will feel the loss, and parents must acknowledge their feelings and help their children work through them. The children's ages will greatly determine the level of understanding and grief that they feel. Our two-year-old was hardly touched by our baby's death, because he had yet to understand that a baby was coming. On the other hand, our five-year-old was deeply saddened and for a long time would randomly say, "Mommy, I wish our baby hadn't died." We took advantage of those times and taught her about God's will for each of our lives, particularly his will to take our baby to heaven.

Each child who is old enough to understand will go through some sort of grieving process. Telling a child not to cry, especially in front of his mother, is an abnormal repression of feelings at a time when the best thing for a child to do is cry. Never embarrass a grieving child. At the very least, engulf him in your arms and cry together reassuring him of your love. Talk freely with him about his sibling. This death is a loss out of his young life, as well. Sometimes when a sibling dies after a lengthy illness, a child may experience guilt over the death because of feeling glad that the death finally came. He must understand that it was not the death for which he was glad, but rather the relief that closed an unpleasant chapter in the family's life.

Now that our family is complete, it has been interesting that the older children realize the impact that the deaths of those earlier children play on the make-up of our family. They often ask me to rehearse the time frame and give details about each of our losses. I believe it is their way of grieving for the siblings they never knew.

Grandparents also need to be a part of the grieving process. They have not only the death of a grandchild to deal with but also the pain of seeing their own child go through something so terrible. Crying together and openly sharing the loss lessens the weight for everyone. This is not the time to keep anyone at arm's length, especially those who love you so dearly. Let them do what they can to help you. It probably is their way of coping with the hurt that they are feeling deeply, as well.

Although not affected as much as your immediate family, your extended family will also feel the pain you are going through. They too will not only grieve your loss but will grieve for you. However, with miles often separating adult siblings, it is almost impossible for them to be at your side during the crucial days following your baby's death. Over a thousand miles separate me from my only sister, Melanie. She sent flowers and called often, and those times of talking to her and crying with her over the phone were a helpful release of emotion for me. Be content with phone calls and other expressions of comfort at this time, and know that other family members are hurting with you and praying for you too.

Grief's Summary

While a loss will affect each person differently, each person affected must deal with his or her loss through a process of grieving. For some, that process may be very short; for others, it may be lengthy. God created each person differently, not only physically but also emotionally. My grieving process, though helpful and healing for me, is not the prescription for every grieving mom. My husband's certainly would not have worked for me, nor mine for him. I cannot spell out for you how to grieve, but I urge you to allow yourself time to grieve, no matter when your loss occurred. As you endure the emotional rollercoaster of the stages of grief—denial, anger, bargaining, depression, and acceptance—[2], recognize God's sovereign hand, accept the peace and comfort that

He desires for you, and look to your future with a renewed hope of what good things He has awaiting you.

He heals the brokenhearted And binds up their wounds.
Psalm 147:3

Does God Care?

*D*oes God really care? Yes, God does care, much more than any of us can possibly imagine. A song that has been a blessing to me, although difficult sometimes to sing, is *Does Jesus Care?* by Frank E. Graeff. I think Reverend Graeff summed it up perfectly as he posed the same question and then answered with a definitive YES. The fourth verse asks, "Does Jesus care when I've said good-bye to the dearest on earth to me, And my sad heart aches till it nearly breaks—Is it aught to Him? Does He see?" The chorus then answers, "O yes, He cares—I know He cares, His heart is touched with my grief; When the days are weary, the long nights dreary, I know my Savior cares."

In the Bible, Hebrews 4:14-16 identifies Christ as our High Priest to whom we can *boldly* come in time of need: "Seeing then that we have a great High Priest who has passed through the heavens, Jesus the Son of God, let us hold fast our confession. For we do not have a High Priest who cannot sympathize with our weaknesses, but was in all points tempted as we are, yet without sin. Let us therefore come boldly to the throne of grace, that we may obtain mercy and find grace to help in time of need." What comes to mind when told to do something with boldness? I think of doing it with confidence, courage, assurance, bravery. So put into that verse these synonyms or whatever came to your mind and go confidently, courageously, and with assurance into Christ's presence where your help awaits.

Not only are we told to come boldly to God, but our relationship to God as a hurting child is depicted in a variety of ways. Ultimately they all lead to God's tender, loving care. In II Peter 5:7 we are told to cast our cares on the Lord because he cares for us. Over and over, the Psalmist describes God as his shield, defender, buckler, and stronghold. Other scriptures refer to our relationship with Christ as a shepherd with his sheep. How aptly we can interpret his care and concern for us as one of his little lambs. Right now, I know, it is hard to fathom that God really cares for you, but he does infinitely more than you can ever imagine. He longs to carry you through this difficulty if you will just let him.

During the middle of a crisis, if we can just remember that God loves us and only brings things into our lives to better fashion us for his service, then we can begin experiencing the hope of the deep care he has for us. God is not in heaven planning how he can make our lives more miserable. On the contrary, he is, planning how he can mold and make us more like himself. The molding process is painful. The firing process more than we desire. Yet still as the clay, we certainly have no right to tell God, the Master Potter, how to create his masterpiece. And that is exactly what each of us will be someday as we stand before God—a masterpiece molded and shaped through the testings and trials of our lives. Proverbs 17:3 tells us, "The refining pot is for silver and the furnace for gold, But the Lord tests the hearts." Whether we shine as gold on the Judgment Day or still look like a rough clay pot is determined now by our acceptance or rejection of these trials. My dear grieving friend, during the midst of your trial, it will be difficult to accept and acknowledge God's sovereign design through it; but it is during the trying heat of the fire that He wants to comfort and sustain you.

Many well-intentioned comforters attempt to help those who are grieving by quoting Romans 8:28: "And we know that all things work together for good to those who love God, to those who are the called according to His purpose" or I Thessalonians 5:18: "in everything give thanks; for this is the will of God in Christ Jesus for you." While they truly are seeking to help, they will probably not understand that these verses comfort very little in the middle of a crisis. It is only after the crisis that we can truly come to a deeper understanding of each of those verses. Romans 8:28 can comfort when we are willing to accept that everything that does come into our lives is the will of God and that it will eventually bring about good. I struggled with this as well as with I Thessalonians 5:18 until I realized that I did not have to be thankful that God took my baby, but I did have to be thankful for the experience and the things learned in the process. There is a difference between being thankful in and being thankful for. So when people make an effort to comfort us, we can graciously accept it and glean from

Scripture the truths about our situation, recognizing that God deeply cares about what has occurred in our lives.

While some teach that a person who has gone through a trial should never ask God why it happened, biblical principles teach us that it is not a sin to ask God why. It is a sin to become bitter because of our possibly never seeing the why answered. For David and Bathsheba, God clearly explained the why through the prophet Nathan. In II Samuel 12:12-14, he says to David, "'For you did it secretly, but I will do this thing before all Israel, before the sun.' So David said to Nathan, 'I have sinned against the Lord.' And Nathan said to David, 'The Lord also has put away your sin; you shall not die. However, because by this deed you have given great occasion to the enemies of the Lord to blaspheme, the child also who is born to you shall surely die.'"

Let me be quick to state here that God does not punish our sin by taking away our children. Christ took the punishment of our sins on himself when he died on the cross ("He himself bore our sins in his body on the tree"—I Peter 2:24 ESV); therefore, the punishment for all the sins of all mankind has already been taken care of. It is now a matter of our accepting Christ's payment for sin for ourselves through salvation. The death of a child is merely the result of living in a world that is full of imperfections and problems and not the punishing hand of God on our lives. However, because of the unique position that David held as the king of God's chosen people, his sin carried with it unique consequences. God's revelation of David's sin forced David to deal with the sin and thus protected the nation of Israel, as well as his testimony as their God.

It is natural and good to do some soul-searching during a trial such as this, but trials do not necessarily mean that there is sin in our lives. In Job 1:1, God calls Job a perfect and upright man, one that feared him and turned away from evil. Yet God let Satan put Job through rigorous testings, which included the deaths of all ten of his children. After my babies' deaths, I didn't just calmly ask God why but rather cried and screamed and begged God to show me why he took my babies. My very patient husband comforted my aching heart with his assurance that God was not using my babies' deaths to punish me. Eventually I accepted losing them as God's will for my life and theirs. Only a few months after my mid-term loss, I was able to minister to a woman who had gone through a similar loss about a month before I had. Shortly thereafter, both she and her husband turned to Christ in salvation. Looking back, I believe the Lord used our baby's death to bring this couple to himself. It is a comfort to establish a possible reason for losing this baby, but I still have no answer as to why God chose to take my other two babies.

Do unanswered whys mean God does not care? No, it simply means he has chosen not to reveal the answers at this time; and we must trust in his great sovereignty more than ever before. Revelation 4:11 which says, "You are worthy, O Lord, To receive glory and honor and power; For You created all things, And by Your will they exist and were created," teaches us that each of our lives, no matter the length, is created and directed by God; and he alone has the absolute right to do whatever he wants with each. My precious babies, though their earthly existence was far shorter than I ever planned, were alive the exact number of days that God planned and through their very short existence here on earth brought glory to their Creator through our testimony of his working all things according to his perfect plan.

Does God care? Absolutely! He cares more than you can imagine at this moment. Yet his care is demonstrated in ways that we find hard to interpret as care; and until we can accept and then cling to Isaiah 55:8-9 and 11-12, we may never fully be able to acknowledge that He really does care.

For My thoughts are not your thoughts, Nor are your ways My ways," says the Lord. For as the heavens are higher than the earth, So are My ways higher than your ways, And My thoughts than your thoughts. For as the rain comes down, and the snow from heaven, And do not return there, But water the earth, And make it bring forth and bud, That it may give seed to the sower And bread to the eater, So shall My word be that goes forth from My mouth; It shall not return to Me void, But it shall accomplish what I please, And it shall prosper in the thing for which I sent it. For you shall go out with joy, And be led out with peace.

Isaiah 55:8-12a

Your Child Now

$\mathcal{W}$henever a baby dies, it is natural for parents to ask, "What caused my baby to die?" Medically, a variety of things happen to cause a little one's death. Depending on the length of the pregnancy, some parents have the benefit of an actual autopsy and closure with a funeral. Others simply have a memorial service, and still others must resume their lives with no finality of good-byes or medical answers. But even more important than parents asking what caused a baby's death, or the death of an older child, is their asking, "Where is my child now?"

I have no doubt that all three of my babies are in Heaven right now, and I fully expect to meet them face to face one day. The Bible does reference parents seeing their children in heaven, and that is in the story of David and Bathsheba. In II Samuel 12:23, David says, "I shall go to him, but he shall not return to me." And that verse, coupled with what we know from the Bible about God's character—that he is gracious and just—leads us to the conclusion that he does not send children to everlasting punishment before they have had a chance to accept or reject His gift of eternal life. Rather, at the time of their death, God takes to heaven with him those children who have not yet reached what many call the "age of accountability."

The age of accountability is when a child understands sin for himself and can acknowledge God's gift of salvation from sin's penalty. For each child, the age of accountability is different. Obviously, a baby in utero has not reached this understanding. Even a toddler who can distinguish right from wrong usually does not comprehend salvation. God, who created your child, is full of mercy and tender compassion. David draws upon this fact in Psalm 51:1 when he is repenting of his sins against Uriah and with Bathsheba. He cries out, "Have mercy upon me, O God, According to Your loving kindness; According to the multitude of Your tender mercies, Blot out my transgressions."

Dear Friend, hold fast to the comfort from God's Word that teaches us that we can see our young children again someday if we have accepted Christ's gift of salvation. What a joyous reunion that will be! But if you have not accepted the gift of salvation and do not know without any doubts or hesitations that you will one day be in heaven, may I encourage you to turn back to the Letter of Introduction right now and read again how you can be sure you will go to heaven when you die?

Because of the sense of hope and comfort it gives, many grieving parents cling to the erroneous belief that their little children become angels after death. However, the Bible clearly teaches some specific things about angels. The first is that they are created beings, just like people are. "Praise Him, all His angels; Praise Him, all His hosts! Let them praise the name of the Lord, For He commanded and they were created" (Psalm 148:2,5). Second, the Bible teaches us that we are not to worship angels. "Let no one cheat you of your reward, taking delight in false humility and worship of angels, intruding into those things which he has not seen, vainly puffed up by his fleshly mind" (Colossians 2:18). And third, the Bible teaches us that angels are separate and distinct from man. "But you have come to Mount Zion and to the city of the living God, the heavenly Jerusalem, to an innumerable company of angels" (Hebrews 12:22).

In the Bible, we also see angels having specific jobs to fulfill. Some are continually around the throne of God worshipping him and proclaiming, "Holy, Holy, Holy." Others, that we call guardian angels, are "ministering spirits." And still others are involved in spiritual warfare.

Our children, like the angels, have a very specific purpose for being in heaven. God creates each individual, and none is in a pre-existent spirit state in heaven prior to conception or becomes an angelic being after death. Your sweet child is now in the very presence of God, fulfilling man's ultimate purpose which is to praise, glorify, and enjoy God for eternity. Your child's death has just allowed him to begin that everlasting purpose sooner, as opposed to later.

This people I have formed for Myself; They shall declare My praise.

Isaiah 43:21

For by Him all things were created that are in heaven and that are on earth, visible and invisible, whether thrones or dominions or principalities or powers. All things were created through Him and for Him.

Colossians 1:16

Thou art worthy, O Lord, to receive glory and honour and power: for thou hast created all things, and for thy pleasure they are and were created.

Revelation 4:11 KJV

Healing — Physical and Emotional

*A*side from the emotional pain, dealing with a post-partum body after either a miscarriage or the loss of an infant at birth is one of the hardest things a mother endures. Unfortunately, for some women who suffer a miscarriage and for those who lose a child at birth, their bodies do not realize the loss that has occurred. Engorgement in preparation for nursing, the pain and discomforts that accompany the normal healing process, and a tummy that is larger than normal—all without a baby—make a very unpleasant and difficult equation. Our bodies change quickly in anticipation of a baby, but they seem to take on a snail's pace in getting back to normal after a tragic loss.

When I miscarried at ten weeks and questioned whether my milk would come in, my doctor told me that each woman's body responds to a miscarriage differently. After our mid-term loss at twenty weeks, I had several occasions, where after hearing a baby cry, I experienced the sensation that I needed to nurse my baby. It was during these times of natural yet difficult responses that I especially had to rely on the Lord and claim verses like Psalm 55:22: "Cast your burden on the Lord, And He shall sustain you"; and I Corinthians 10:13: "No temptation [or trial] has over-taken you except such as is common to man; but God is faithful, who will not allow you to be tempted [tried] beyond what you are able."

After a pregnancy has ended, a mother's body must also endure the painful healing process, which includes bleeding.

For most women, this takes about four to six weeks; but every day of those weeks of healing can be an agonizing reminder of what happened. Because this healing process lasted much longer for me, my doctor finally intervened medically. If the post-partum pain or healing process seems to become lengthy or overwhelming at any point, consult your physician for options that are available for you. With today's medical advances, no mom needs to suffer unnecessarily at an already difficult time.

Physical exercise, as approved by a doctor, does help immensely. Taking a long walk each day to be alone with the Lord or with your spouse to talk about all that has happened benefits the physical body, as well as the emotions. Just as engorgement reminds the mother of what should have been a happy time, so a round stomach is a reminder of the baby she carried. Therefore, exercising to flatten the tummy is just as necessary as controlling physical discomforts caused by the pregnancy loss. As soon as you are physically able, get out of your house and get yourself going again. The fresh air and change of scenery will do wonders to boost your spirits. The sooner you feel good about your body again, the sooner you will have a more positive outlook in other areas, as well.

God uniquely designed a woman's body, yet it can be a very frustrating creation. Take heart, Dear One, you will feel "normal" again in time. Be willing to give yourself the time that you need, though; and keep trusting the God

Who says, "My grace is sufficient for you, for My strength is made perfect in weakness" (II Corinthians 12:9).

A Word about Depression

Women who go through a normal pregnancy that ends in a safe delivery of a healthy baby can go through post-partum depression ("baby blues"), due to multiple hormonal changes. So much more susceptible is a woman who has experienced the sudden cessation of a pregnancy or the mom who has carried full term but now has no baby to hold. The feeling of utter despair without a sense of purpose can become very real in a short amount of time. Some symptoms that may point to post-partum depression include extreme sadness, unexplained fatigue, insomnia, appetite changes, crying episodes, anxiety, irritability, isolation, and even thoughts of suicide. If you are experiencing any of these symptoms or any other non-characteristic behaviors for you, please seek the help of others. Your spouse, pastor, pastor's wife, and doctor are all allies that want to help you heal emotionally, as well as physically. But most of all, the Lord wants to give you hope at this time. Philippians 4:6-7 tells us to "Be anxious for nothing, but in everything by prayer and supplication, with thanksgiving, let your requests be made known unto God; And the peace of God, which surpasses all understanding, will guard your hearts and minds through Christ Jesus."

Why are you cast down, O my soul? And why are you disquieted within me? Hope in God; For I shall yet praise Him, The help of my countenance and my God.

Psalm 43:5

Going on from Here

The thought of going on with life, getting back into a routine, and even enjoying life again, may bring waves of guilt and seem like an impossibility; but "going on" does not mean forgetting about a child or ignoring feelings of deep pain. It does mean loosening the grip on those feelings a little bit in order to get things into perspective.

One of the first steps to going on is to give up all of the what-ifs. My what-ifs list was long. A few were: What if I had just noticed a change in movement? What if I had paid more attention to that unusual pain? What if I had called my doctor sooner? What if I had just gone on to the hospital? What if that activity hadn't been part of my day? Every what-if question is just a straw at which we grasp to try to make our loss a little easier to bear. More often than not, though, our what-ifs just cause us more guilt and pain. With God, though, there are no what-ifs. Everything is absolute, and he carries out his will no matter what we do or do not do. So when we entertain those what-if thoughts, we must turn them over to the Lord and accept and surrender the circumstances as God's will for our lives.

Another step to take in going on is to do something as a remembrance or memorial for your baby. An acquaintance deeply touched my heart when she sent a pressed rose in a card to me. She said in her card that she and her husband had pressed one in memory of their baby that they had lost, and so she did one in memory of our baby. Of course, I cried; but that rose will always be special to me. You can remember your children in many different ways, like writing a letter to say good-bye (see Additional Helps) or giving a donation in their memory to your church or another charity. As a family, we planted three trees on our church's property. After our first miscarriage, I chose a simple piece of jewelry, a ring with a stone depicting the month of our baby's due date. After our second loss, I changed the stone to a less specific one, and still to this day wear it not as a memorial or "shrine" to my children but as a reminder that they were each a very special gift from God—a gift that deeply touched my heart, was with me for only a short time, but changed my life forever. You must decide for yourself what will be a comfort and a way to begin closing this chapter of your life. It will be a concrete step toward turning loose and going on.

One of the best steps to take in going on is to claim a promise from Scripture. Doing so can give great comfort and courage. Shortly after our second baby died, I came across II Corinthians 4:17-18, which says, "For our light affliction, which is but for a moment, is working for us a far more exceeding and eternal weight of glory, while we do not look at the things which are seen, but at the things which are not seen. For the things which are seen are temporary, but the things which are not seen are eternal." After showing it to my husband, we decided to put that verse on all our thank you notes and correspondence regarding the baby so that others would know that our trust was in the

Lord. If you do not know how to find verses of promise and encouragement, take some time to read through the compilation of encouraging verses found in the Additional Helps section. Perhaps one will be just what you need to hold fast to right now.

For some couples, a good prescription for going on is deciding to have another baby. We know that David and Bathsheba went on to have more children together. In fact, in spite of their infamous sin, the Lord was gracious to bless their union with Solomon, the wisest and possibly most famous king in Israel's history.

If another pregnancy is possible, do not let others pressure you into something for which you are not ready. Only you will know if and when you are ready. Because your body does need time to recover, do not make a hasty decision, hoping another pregnancy will help mend your broken heart. On the other hand, by completely closing the door on the subject, you may rob yourself of God's special blessing for your family. You will have fears to overcome; yet with God's help you can face another pregnancy with peace, joy, and great anticipation, knowing that God is always in control and that whatever happens through that pregnancy is in his hands as well.

If another pregnancy is simply not an option for medical or other reasons, then consider whether the Lord would have you and your husband adopt a baby. Just like those who decide to pursue another pregnancy, you must also be the one to decide if this is the road down which you are prepared to travel. Regardless of whether or not you pursue having another child, I would encourage you to be around other babies as soon as possible. Just holding a little one may feel like a knife in your heart to begin with (it certainly did for me); but sooner than you may think, it will feel good to hold a baby.

Another uncertainty that many women deal with when trying to move on after a miscarriage, especially if they do not have any other children, is the haunting question, "Am I a mother or not?" Absolutely! Because life begins at conception, so does motherhood. Every year our church gives a small gift to the mothers in attendance on Mother's Day. One of these mothers is an elderly lady who had two miscarriages prior to her husband's very early death. I always tell her, "Happy Mother's Day," and make sure she takes a gift, because I know that otherwise she would not take one or have anyone acknowledge that she is a mother. She annually reminds me that she does not have any children, and I annually remind her that she does—in heaven, waiting to meet her!

Going on is definitely easier said than done. Give yourself a lot of time, but do not mourn your life away either. Listen to your body, your emotions, and the Lord; all three will work together to make you ready for daily life once again.

Weeping may endure for a night, But joy comes in the morning.

Psalm 30:5

But I will hope continually, And will praise You yet more and more.

Psalm 71:14

Helping Others

*W*hen we lost our second child, we received many phone calls, cards, and letters. We appreciated all of them, because each one indicated that someone was praying for us. The ones that touched me the most, though, were the ones from people who had previously walked in my shoes. They, too, had lost a child and knew exactly what I was going through. Some of them related their experiences and made me aware of how gracious God was to me to spare me from similar circumstances. Through them, I learned that in time God could use my losses to help me comfort others.

Second Corinthians 1:3-4 ESV says, "Blessed be the God and Father of our Lord Jesus Christ, the Father of mercies and God of all comfort, who comforts us in all our affliction, so that we may be able to comfort those who are in any affliction, with the comfort with which we ourselves are comforted by God." These verses teach us that we can be a comfort to others just by sharing with them our experience and how the Lord helped us through it. While that may seem simplistic, hearing our situation and our praise to God may be exactly what others need to hear. It will also bring glory to the Lord. As he grants us physical and emotional healing, we will find ourselves being able to minister in more specific ways to other hurting people.

One tremendous avenue of help is prayer. What a blessing it was to receive those cards that affirmed that someone else was praying for us! The faithful prayers of friends and family helped us through those hard times in ways that I still do not completely understand.

Intercessory prayer is a wonderful journey on which to embark for someone hurting with an all-too-familiar pain. By recalling some of our most difficult struggles like the extreme emotions, physical healing, emptiness, discouragement, depressions, and anger, we can pray specifically and more fervently for others.

Some practical ways we can help are by preparing meals for the hurting family, watching their other children, cleaning their house, or running errands for them. Each would be a way to comfort during a difficult time. If the hurting family refuses the services we offer, we should give them a little more time to heal and then offer our help again later.

Above all, we must never shy away from a grieving mother because of our thinking we do not know what to say. A kind hug and an "I understand" says much more than a whole conversation, as you have probably already found to be true.

C. H. Spurgeon sums it up beautifully, "When your faith endures many conflicts and your spirit sinks low, do not condemn yourself. There is a reason for your season of heaviness. Great soldiers are not made without war. Skillful sailors are not trained on the shore. It appears that if you are to become a great believer you will be greatly tested. If you are to be a great helper to others, you must pass through their trials. The uncut diamond has little brilliance, the unthreshed corn feeds no one, and the untried believer is of little use or beauty. There are great benefits to come from your trials."[3]

We cannot go wrong by offering help and words of hope and comfort from our personal experiences, but the most important thing to offer a grieving friend is the hope and comfort that can only come through Jesus Christ, "the God of all comfort."

Blessed is the man who trusts in the Lord, And whose hope is the Lord.

Jeremiah 17:7

Closing

I trust that *Hope for a Mom's Heart* has in some way helped ease the pain of your child's death. While writing it, I felt the weight of my own loss lessen somewhat, as if others were now helping bear it.

The idea of writing something like this came about after my first miscarriage. But it took hearing about the death of a two-day-old baby boy years later to start the flow of words onto paper. My heart broke for the parents who are missionaries in a foreign country. After many years of marriage, they were eagerly anticipating their first child. I certainly cannot understand God's decision to take their baby at birth; but in crying out to the Lord for them, he seemed to motivate me to start writing. I know the Lord has given these missionaries the strength to carry on for him, just as he has done for me. They now have two children through adoption. For some reason, my third miscarriage sent my book to the back burner to simmer for many more years. Every time I heard about a family dealing with the loss of a baby, I would pray for them and wish there was more that I could do to help. Through the Lord's continued promptings, direction, and certainly His grace, maybe now with *Hope for a Mom's Heart*, God is allowing me to help in a small way.

Dear Reader, may God be especially close to you at this time and give you the comfort, peace, and hope that you need.

May you be "looking unto Jesus the author and finisher of our faith," (Hebrews 12:2) and may "The Lord bless you and keep you; The Lord make His face shine upon you, And be gracious to you; The Lord lift up His countenance upon you, And give you peace" (Numbers 6:24-26).

And finally, "May the God of hope fill you with all joy and peace in believing, so that by the power of the Holy Spirit you may abound in hope." (Romans 15:13 ESV).

Merri Ellen

You may contact Merri Ellen at
www.hopeforamomsheart.tateauthor.com

Additional Helps

God's Plan of Salvation
Our Only Hope of Heaven

Heaven is a free gift.

The free gift of God is eternal life in Christ Jesus our Lord. Romans 6:23 ESV

For by grace you have been saved through faith. And this is not your own doing; it is the gift of God, not of works, lest anyone should boast. Ephesians 2:8-9 ESV

Everyone is a sinner.

But we are all like an unclean thing, And all our righteousnesses are like filthy rags. Isaiah 64:6

As it is written: "There is none righteous, no, not one. Romans 3:10

For all have sinned and fall short of the glory of God. Romans 3:23

The consequence of sin is death.

For the wages of sin is death. Romans 6:23

Without the shedding of blood there is no forgiveness of sins. Hebrews 9:22

And as it is appointed for men to die once, but after this the judgment. Hebrews 9:27

Jesus paid the penalty for sin with His own blood.

For God so loved the world that He gave His only begotten Son, that whoever believes in Him should not perish but have everlasting life. John 3:16

But God shows his love for us in that while we were still sinners, Christ died for us. Romans 5:8 ESV

Moreover, brethren, I declare to you the gospel ... 2 by which also you are saved, 3 For I delivered to you first of all that which I also received: that Christ died for our sins according to the Scriptures, 4 and that He was buried, and that He rose again the third day according to the Scriptures. I Corinthians 15:1-4

In whom we have redemption through His blood, the forgiveness of sins. Colossians 1:14

We accept God's gift of Heaven by placing our faith in what Jesus did on the cross.

"Sirs, what must I do to be saved?" So they said, "Believe on the Lord Jesus Christ, and you will be saved, you and your household." Acts 16:30-31

For with the heart one believes and is justified, and with the mouth one confesses and is saved Romans 10:10 ESV.

For whoever calls on the name of the Lord shall be saved. Romans 10:13

All of these verses should point you to Jesus Christ who, as I said at the outset, came to the earth with one purpose in mind—to take on himself the punishment of every person's sin so that all of mankind could spend eternity with him in Heaven forever. By believing in faith that his payment for your sins is sufficient for your salvation. You receive his salvation by simply talking to him through a prayer such as this:

> Dear God, I know that I am a sinner, and I understand that my sin will separate me from you for all of eternity. I am asking for your forgiveness of

my sins, and I am accepting your death on the cross, your burial, and your resurrection as the payment that purchased a place in heaven for me. Thank you for this wonderful gift of salvation. Amen.

If you prayed this prayer in faith, believing that Christ has saved you, please share with me this wonderful news through my website at www.hopeforamomsheart. tateauthor.com.

Medical Questions and Answers

*A*ny type of pregnancy loss brings with it many medical questions. I have tried to compile a list of some of the questions I had after my losses, as well as some questions hurting moms have asked me. This list is in no way exhaustive, yet I trust it will be helpful. Your doctor should be the ultimate source of information for your specific situation; but in general, these answers may give you some peace of mind or direction right now.

I must express a very special thank you to Dr. Joy Welsh, my gynecologist and my friend, who patiently went through these questions with me and supplied medical answers for you. Though she never walked through a loss with me, she has expressed from the first day we met an understanding and concern for women facing such heartache. Even though over the span of her career she has seen many miscarriages and deaths of infants, she has not allowed herself to become calloused to the hurt that accompanies each. She eagerly accepted my invitation to share her medical expertise so that many women can benefit from medical answers concerning what they have just experienced, are going through now, or may be facing in the very near future.

Q: How early in a pregnancy can a miscarriage be diagnosed?

A: A fetal heartbeat can be visualized on an ultrasound as early as six weeks. If the heartbeat is not seen, another ultrasound will be administered in two weeks, in case the dates are off. At that time, a miscarriage can be confirmed.

Q: What are some warning signs of miscarriage?

A: Vaginal spotting, cramping, and if previously present, the loss of breast tenderness and morning sickness, are all soft indications of possible fetal demise.

Q: Does "spotting" always mean a miscarriage is occurring?

A: No, many women spot in the first trimester, especially at the time when the fertilized egg implants in the uterus.

Q: If a woman or her doctor thinks a miscarriage is occurring, is there anything either can do to prevent it?

A: Some early miscarriages are associated with a low progesterone level in the first trimester. This is related to a luteal phase defect where not enough progesterone is produced. This causes the uterine lining to break down causing menstruation. (For more information, go to www.early-pregnancy-tests.com/lutealphasedefect. html.) If tested early enough, one can be given progesterone to raise the levels to normal range, sustaining the pregnancy. Past this point, if a pregnancy is miscarrying in the first trimester, there is nothing that can be done. God and nature are in control.

Q: At what point should a mother seek medical attention regarding concerns about her pregnancy?

A: If a woman is having spotting and cramping, she should contact her physician.

Q: What type of tests will be given to determine if a miscarriage is occurring?

A: An ultrasound will be done to confirm fetal viability. Blood work may also be done to test the levels of the pregnancy hormone HCG. The level doubles every forty-eight hours in a normal pregnancy.

Q: Is an ultrasound usually accurate?

A: If a woman is off on her cycle dates, then she may not be as far along in her pregnancy as she thought. In this instance, the heartbeat may not yet be visualized. But with accurate dates, the ultrasound is accurate in determining fetal viability.

Q: What are some reasons that miscarriages occur?

A: Most miscarriages happen because the fetus is not developing correctly or because of a genetic abnormality.

Q: What are some reasons that stillbirths occur?

A: Stillbirths can occur because of in utero infections, genetic abnormalities, or cord accidents (when the umbilical cord wraps around the fetal neck or when a knot in the cord tightens).

Q: What are some reasons that infant deaths occur?
A: Infection, genetic abnormalities.

Q: Can taking over-the-counter medications cause a miscarriage?
A: No.

Q: Does age factor into miscarriages, and how old is too old to get pregnant?
A: One in four pregnancies miscarries. As women age, they do have a slightly higher risk of miscarriage and of genetic abnormalities in pregnancies. At the age of thirty five, women are offered the option of a genetic amniocentesis to determine any genetic abnormalities. As long as a woman is ovulating, she theoretically is able to conceive.

Q: If a woman previously had an abortion, does that raise her chances of miscarriage?
A: If there were any complications with the abortion, or if there was any damage to the cervix, there might be an increased chance of miscarriage in subsequent pregnancies. However, most uneventful first-trimester abortions carry no increased chances of future miscarriages.

Q: Can a woman "overdo it" and cause a miscarriage?
A: No.

Q: Does being "out of shape" or overweight have any bearing on having a miscarriage?
A: There have been studies that do indicate an increase of infertility in obese women; but overall, neither being "out of shape" nor overweight holds any miscarriage consequences.

Q: Can an emotionally negative attitude about being pregnant cause a physical response of miscarriage?
A: Absolutely not.

Q: Does having sexual intercourse while pregnant put the life of the baby in danger?
A: In a pregnancy that is progressing normally, sexual intercourse can continue. A couple can enjoy intimacy; this will not harm the ongoing pregnancy.

Q: To what degree does the father's genetics factor into a miscarriage?
A: The father's genetics factor into a miscarriage only if he passes on a genetic defect that is incompatible with life.

Q: What exactly is happening, from a medical perspective, when a miscarriage is occurring?

A: A miscarriage is occurring when the fetus (baby) has died; and the uterus is sloughing or ridding itself of the tissue and the placenta.

Q: Is a D&C really necessary?

A: Many women and their physicians choose to let nature take its course and allow the miscarriage to occur naturally. (The blood loss from a spontaneous miscarriage and that from a D&C are fairly equal.) Some women choose to have a D&C, rather than wait up to several weeks to spontaneously miscarry.

Q: What can a woman expect her body to do after a miscarriage?

A: A woman will usually have a menstrual cycle four weeks after a miscarriage. If she had regular cycles before the pregnancy, her cycle should continue normally.

Q: How soon after a miscarriage can a woman get pregnant again?

A: Because the miscarriage acts like a period, a woman will ovulate approximately two weeks after the miscarriage. She could get pregnant at that time; however it is recommended that she wait for one or two normal periods before trying again to conceive. This allows her body time to get back to normal after the miscarriage.

Q: What are the chances of miscarriages happening one right after another?

A: Unless there is a genetic problem, a woman will usually have a normal pregnancy after a miscarriage.

Q: Is there medication or vitamins that can help a woman carry her baby to term?

A: Every pregnant woman should eat a healthy diet and take prenatal vitamins as recommended by her caregiver.

Q: Is there any way for a woman to prepare her body for another pregnancy?

A: Yes, she should make sure she is in good health—no smoking, taking drugs, or drinking alcohol; maintaining a healthy weight; and regularly getting enough sleep.

Q: Is there a point when a woman should give up trying to have a baby?

A: This is something she will need to discuss with her physician, especially if she has a medical problem that puts her life or health in danger with a pregnancy.

Others Understand

You may be feeling all alone right now, but you are not. Many women have walked in your shoes and found that the Lord turned their blisters into calluses, enabling them to walk on with him. I have invited several women with different situations to share their personal account of loss yet gain. I trust their openness will be a blessing to you, as well as an encouragement in realizing that others do understand.

Debbi Gray

My experience with losing my second child started with a normal, complication-free pregnancy. The baby was pretty active. She seemed to like to roll more than anything. I asked a midwife at one of my checkups, "What keeps the baby from getting tangled up in the cord?" She seemed unconcerned and said the baby pulled it along behind him or her.

The events of our tragic weekend started with the baby rolling on Thursday night—the last movement I remember. On Friday, I had a routine checkup with a midwife; and at first, she couldn't find a heartbeat with the device they use so the mom can hear it, too. She used a special stethoscope and thought she found it with that. Later in the day, I realized that I couldn't remember feeling any movement the entire day. I had no reason to think there was anything wrong. I had just had a checkup. I shoved any uneasiness back in my mind. On Saturday, I periodically felt a pushing sensation, which I now know were contractions. I called the doctor's office because I was concerned that I hadn't felt any other movement. I was told to drink some juice and lie down. I did that and called back to say that all I felt was the pushing sensation. Still no one seemed alarmed. Late Saturday night, after having uncomfortable contractions that were five minutes apart, I went to the hospital to be checked. The nurse measured the contractions and began to look for a heartbeat. She couldn't find one but didn't seem worried, saying that sometimes the baby was turned the wrong way. But then the doctor on call came in with an ultrasound machine to see if he could find a heartbeat. He found the baby's chest cavity, but there was no heartbeat. He tried to put a scalp monitor on the baby but couldn't. He was very compassionate and said he didn't understand what had happened. When it finally sank in that our baby was dead, I asked that she be delivered by c-section. Because our pastor was out of the country on a mission trip, our assistant pastor came and prayed with us before I went to surgery. He stayed with my husband the rest of the night. Around two or three in the morning on Sunday, our little Alyssa Caryn was born just a few days before her due date. Her cause of death—the cord was wrapped tightly around her neck three times.

When I came out of recovery, a nurse came to ask if I wanted to hold my baby. I wanted to but was concerned about how she would look. The nurses had taken several pictures of her for me, and they let me see those just before they brought her in. She was so precious, and holding her was very difficult, but knowing she was with the Lord was a big comfort. The Lord gave me and my husband grace and a peace I can't describe! We were able to use Alyssa's death as a testimony to nurses and others we came in contact with. We told them that the Lord was helping us through this difficult time. Our assistant pastor and his wife were such a blessing to us. Because my husband was very shaken by the loss of Alyssa and couldn't drive, our assistant pastor took him home to shower and change clothes. His wife came and sat by my bed while he was away. Friends and family came to visit, and I found that talking about what had happened really helped to ease the hurt.

Right away, I said I wanted another baby; so about six months later I was pregnant again. At sixteen weeks, I started bleeding. I knew I was losing another baby. A visit to the doctor's office confirmed that I was having a miscarriage. This time I told my husband, "I don't know if I can go through this again." Our pastor came to visit and said he knew we probably felt the Lord didn't want us to have any more children but not to feel that way.

It didn't take me long to decide I wanted to try again. And try we did for two years without success. It seemed that everywhere I looked there were babies or pregnant women. I hurt inside when I'd see them. I prayed and prayed that the Lord would give us a strong healthy baby, and he did finally bless us with another daughter. She has brought a lot of joy to our home!

I do understand what you are going through! Please know that God's grace is sufficient. He has proven himself faithful to us many times!

Lisa Shelhorse

I had never been so tired in my life. I made Christmas cookies for a Christmas party and then was too tired to attend it. I was sure I was pregnant for the first time, but my menstrual period came and went and I assumed I had been wrong. Later after some unusual bleeding and cramping, my pregnancy was confirmed. Unfortunately, I heard the doctor speaking in her office hallway about the possibility of my having a miscarriage somewhere down the road.

Days passed, and then I learned that I had an ectopic or tubal pregnancy and needed surgery. I really felt betrayed by God. He knew how much I wanted a baby. I was finally pregnant and then it was all taken away. What if I couldn't have children? I felt emotionally numb and alone for awhile. When my menstrual cycles returned, they brought great depression with them. I truly believe Satan used my physical weakness to get a hold in my life.

Then one day I got angry with God, because I was afraid I wasn't going to get what I wanted. I doubted God's will and love for me, and I was totally miserable. After a few hours of pouting and being angry, I finally surrendered.

First, I confessed my sins of doubt, fear, and anger. Second, I gave up my desires for God's. I yielded and accepted whatever life God had for me, children or no children (which was very hard). Next I told the Lord that independent, strong Lisa could not make it alone. I had to depend on his help. Peace returned. Strangely, I didn't even want to conceive the next month (though permitted by my doctor). I wanted to see God's work.

Praise God! That month I had no physical or emotional pain. The Lord was so good to me. He answered more than one prayer. The following month I became pregnant and then delivered a beautiful boy. Two years later the Lord gave me a darling little girl. Even with two wonderful kids, I'll never forget the little one I have in heaven.

First Corinthians 15:57 says, "But thanks be to God, who gives us the victory through our Lord Jesus Christ."

Karen Wooster

At twenty-three weeks of pregnancy, an ultrasound showed difficulty of major proportion for my child. A neural tube defect called Encephalocle, in which the baby's brain was forming abnormally, had been detected. With seventeen weeks remaining until the due date, we were told that our child would probably not live through delivery, or at best might live a day, a week, or a month. Only God could provide strength, rest, and guidance for the months ahead.

Initially I began to ponder what hopes would not be realized for my son David. My thoughts were then directed towards God's purpose—that each of my children might glorify the Lord. Later I realized that God accomplished this goal through David's brief life.

God is faithful. His presence, power, and peace are abundant in times of trials. Isaiah 26:3 says, "You will keep him in perfect peace, whose mind is stayed on You, Because he trusts in You." Dealing with my emotions was the biggest challenge. To deal with these intense emotions and the extended process of grief, I determined to set my focus on God. Realizing that God intended a life of joy and victory, I allowed myself to cry but immediately followed these times with reading the Bible, focusing on one specific reason to praise the Lord, and then praying.

David arrived nineteen weeks later and lived one day. Certainly it was a difficult and painful situation. Yet I realized that God was in control, and he knew what was best. I learned to praise God, regardless of my circumstances. I still don't know why this trial was brought into my life. It isn't the path I would choose, but I'm not sure I would want the situation changed either. There is a sweetness to the times of drawing close to the Lord through trials.

Kristy Wright, my sister-in-law

As I look back over my life, the good hand of God is so evident. Although the years have been full of joy and great blessing, there have been times of darkness and deep trials. One such time occurred about twenty years ago. After my husband and I had been married about three years, we found out that we were expecting our first child. Shortly after receiving this good news, I miscarried. I experienced many of the various emotions common to this experience with the predominant emotion being fear—fear of what was going on with my body and fear that I would never be able to have a child. The Lord saw us through this trial; and shortly after, I conceived and bore our first and only son. We were then blessed with two precious daughters.

Our children were so dear to us, and we desired greatly to have more. God had a different plan. After our last daughter was born, I had four more miscarriages. This was a time of much grief and sorrow, but God was present with us. Many times throughout this period of my life, I was directed to Psalm 34. Through this Psalm, God reminded me that he is ever present no matter what the circumstance, he has the power to sustain me through even the most difficult trials, and that his plan for me is always good. "The LORD is near to the brokenhearted and saves the crushed in spirit." Psalm 34:18 ESV

Ranya Huffman

On Monday, March 4, 2002, my husband Steven and I found out that we were expecting twins! Even though I am a twin, I was surprised, because I thought twins skipped a generation. I was thrilled with the idea of having these two babies but also a little overwhelmed, because I already had a four-year-old girl, Ashlyn, and a twenty-month old boy, Austin. At age thirty-one, I had the privilege of being a homemaker and a help to my husband who served as an assistant pastor at our church.

After hearing the news of our expecting twins, my doctor asked me to come back two weeks later for a follow-up ultrasound; and on March 18, his suspicion of a problem with one of the twins was confirmed. Three weeks to the day after the news of twins, we found ourselves at the office of a maternal-fetal specialist. We officially had a problem with Twin A. The doctor told us that part of our daughter's brain was missing and that her spinal cord was not properly developed. He thought our daughter would be handicapped. Our hearts were overwhelmed with fear and grief as we faced the biggest trial of our almost nine years of marriage. As a Christian and pastor's wife, I should have been able to handle this trial, but I was struggling with God's plan for our lives.

Waiting rooms and doctor visits became a regular part of my life as we monitored the progress of Twin A and her problems and the progress of Twin B, in an effort to maintain her good health. Even though my life was in the public eye, at the time I did not want everyone to know the problem I was facing. My husband and I do not believe in abortion, and we were committed to avoiding one, but it seemed like it would have been an "easy" fix. I am thankful that our specialist was a Christian and supported us in this decision.

Until the baby was born, I wrestled with a fear of the unknown. I wanted Twin A to be healthy, but deep down I knew it was not going to happen. It was during this time that the promise of Isaiah 26:3 was a real encouragement to me: "You will keep him in perfect peace, whose mind is stayed on You, Because he trusts in You." God used this verse to give me a peace that we were going to get through this trial.

On Monday, July 15, I was having another routine visit with my specialist. Our twins were due on August 15, but the doctors decided not to wait that long to take the babies, because Twin B was not gaining enough weight. Our plans changed quickly. My husband put off a week of school in his doctoral program, and family came in from out of town for my c-section the next day. On Tuesday, July 16, 2002, at 12:52 in the afternoon, Aubrey Rachelle Huffman (Twin A) was born. She gave a short cry, and immediately needed medical attention. She weighed 4 pounds, 10 ounces, and was 15 3/4 inches long. Autumn Renee Huffman (Twin B) was born at 12:54 in the afternoon. She weighed 3 pounds, 14 ounces, and was 16 inches long. The hours ahead found our twin girls in the NICU. Autumn was doing well for a preemie, but Aubrey had to be on life support. Even though Aubrey received excellent medical care, she was not able to breathe on her own. We had to wrestle with the decision of keeping our daughter on life support. The medical doctors were not able to help her. We made the decision to remove her from life support and let her final moments be with the family in our hospital room. She died around eight in the evening on Wednesday, July 17, 2002. God gave Aubrey to us for about thirty-one hours. It was definitely a season of grief and sadness. On Saturday, July 20, we had a sweet viewing and funeral service attended by family and friends.

As we drove away from the funeral, we opened an envelope from a family friend. Inside was a check for one thousand dollars. God was already providing for our needs. Our gracious heavenly Father promises in 1 Corinthians 10:13 that he will not give us more than we can handle. God kept his promise to me. He knew that I would not have been able to handle Aubrey and all her needs had she lived, but that I could handle this trial and the thirty-one hours that I had to be her mom. He also knew that I could handle rearing Autumn. She spent over three weeks at NICU until she could join our family at home, just days before our oldest daughter started kindergarten. The support of my giving family and generous friends helped and encouraged me in the days ahead, and I could not have done it without them. My mother-in-law spent days living with us. Friends provided food. People cleaned my house or drove me to the hospital to see Autumn. Our lawn care was provided free of charge for weeks. Friends and family sent cards of encouragement and money that helped with all the expenses. God was gracious to care for me each step of the way.

For those who wonder how to help in times of loss, a person meeting practical needs was one of the greatest blessings.

As I face the future, there are moments of grief but seasons of joy. My husband and I grew closer together because of this trial and developed a greater compassion for others. I have definitely grieved over the loss of Aubrey; but Autumn, whose name reminds you of a season, provides seasons of joy to our family. She has such a sweet and compassionate spirit. I do not desire to relive the days of 2002; but I know that in similar days in the future, God's grace will be sufficient during seasons of both joy and grief.

Bruce and Rella Wright, my in-laws

(I interviewed them and then wrote the following about my husband's brother Gary.)

Like many unexpected pregnancies, the surprise gives way to excitement and anticipation by both the parents and the older siblings. This was the case when my husband's family first learned that a fourth child would be joining their family. Gary Wayne Wright, a seemingly healthy baby boy, was born on February 16, 1971.

Apart from being a fussy baby who was very hard to keep content, Gary seemed to develop normally until he was about four months old. Rella was concerned, though, because he was not rolling over or smiling. She recalls holding Gary one time before she knew that something was gravely wrong with him. He made eye contact with her, which was rare, and smiled. She commented at the time to her own mother that she had just gotten a "golden smile." Only a short time later did she realize what a priceless treasure that smile really was.

At a four-and-a-half-month checkup, the doctor misdiagnosed that Gary's fussiness was a result of his being spoiled. However at his six-month checkup, the doctor changed his opinion and recognized that something was very wrong. After eight grueling days of testing in Morgantown, West Virginia, which was about an hour and a half away from their home in West Milford, West Virginia, Gary was diagnosed with a rare and fatal degenerative disorder called Krabbe's-Leukodystrophy. No treatment was available, and the doctors really were not sure how long Gary would live. Rella compares hearing that Gary was going to die to that of someone repeatedly stabbing her and twisting the knife with each blow.

At that time, there had only been a few others diagnosed with this same neurological disorder. Krabbe's, also called Globoid Cell Leukodystrophy, is caused by a deficiency of galactocerebrosidase (GALC), an essential enzyme for myelin metabolism. Without this enzyme, toxins build up in the brain, eventually affecting all neurological and motor functions of the body. This causes the regression of normal development and skills and usually takes a baby's life within the first two years. Because of the newness of the disease, the Wrights underwent scores of interviews; and Gary had to endure many testing procedures. At a certain point, for Gary's sake, the Wrights just had to stop the tests.

Life for the Wright family revolved around doing all that was necessary to keep Gary alive. The rewards were few and the heartache great. The Wrights were sure that Gary could recognize certain voices; but toward the end of his life, the doctors diagnosed him as being blind and deaf. On at least one occasion, Bruce had to resuscitate Gary at home. For about the last six months of his life, Gary's only sustenance came from a feeding tube. Due to multiple medical problems that were developing, Gary was frequently admitted to the hospital. The inevitable came about 11:00 p.m. on April 28, 1973: Gary passed away.

The Wright family did not have a church family to uphold them at this difficult time, nor did they have a strong faith in God. However, both Bruce and Rella agree that they had a core belief in the goodness of God and did not blame him or become bitter. Bruce even recalls that he had no doubt that Gary was in Heaven and that if he ever wanted to see him again, he would have to give his life to Christ. Four years after Gary's death, Bruce and Rella, along with their other three children, began attending a local church that had been kind to them through some of the heartache of losing Gary. It was at this church that four of the five family members accepted Christ as their personal Savior (Rella had been saved previously), and all five were baptized together a short time later.

God used this very difficult time in the Wright's family to draw all of them to himself, just as he wants to do for each mother reading this book. God longs to either enter into a relationship with you or deepen the one that he already has with you so that he truly can work all things together for your good through this experience.

He has put a new song in my mouth—Praise to our God; Many will see it and fear, And will trust in the Lord.

Psalm 40:3

He heals the brokenhearted And binds up their wounds. Great is our Lord, and mighty in power; His understanding is infinite.

Psalm 147:3, 5

Verses of Hope & Comfort

Romans 15:4 ESV

... through endurance and through the encouragement of the Scriptures we might have hope.

Psalm 23:1-6

The Lord is my shepherd; I shall not want. 2 He makes me to lie down in green pastures; He leads me beside the still waters. 3 He restores my soul; He leads me in the paths of righteousness For His name's sake. 4 Yea, though I walk through the valley of the shadow of death, I will fear no evil; For You are with me; Your rod and Your staff, they comfort me. 5 You prepare a table before me in the presence of my enemies; You anoint my head with oil; My cup runs over. 6 Surely goodness and mercy shall follow me All the days of my life; And I will dwell in the house of the Lord forever.

Psalm 42:5-6 ESV

Why are you cast down, O my soul, and why are you in turmoil within me? Hope in God; for I shall again praise him, my salvation and my God.

Psalm 46:1-3

God is our refuge and strength, A very present help in trouble. 2 Therefore we will not fear, Even though the earth be removed, And though the mountains be carried into the midst of the sea; 3 Though its waters roar and be troubled, Though the mountains shake with its swelling.

Psalm 46:10-11

Be still, and know that I am God; I will be exalted among the nations, I will be exalted in the earth! 11 The Lord of hosts is with us; The God of Jacob is our refuge.

Psalm 91:15

He shall call upon Me, and I will answer him; I will be with him in trouble; I will deliver him and honor him.

Psalm 121

I will lift up my eyes to the hills—From whence comes my help? 2 My help comes from the Lord, Who made heaven and earth. 3 He will not allow your foot to be moved; He who keeps you will not slumber. 4 Behold, He who keeps Israel shall neither slumber nor sleep. 5 The Lord is your keeper; The Lord is your shade at your right hand. 6 The sun shall not strike you by day, Nor the moon by night. 7 The Lord shall preserve you from all evil; He shall preserve your soul. 8 The Lord shall preserve your going out and your coming in From this time forth, and even forevermore.

Proverbs 3:5-6

Trust in the Lord with all your heart, And lean not on your own understanding; 6 In all your ways acknowledge Him, And He shall direct your paths.

Lamentations 3:32-33

Though He causes grief, Yet He will show compassion According to the multitude of His mercies. 33 For He does not afflict willingly, Nor grieve the children of men.

Isaiah 40:28-31

Have you not known? Have you not heard? The everlasting God, the Lord, The Creator of the ends of the earth, neither faints nor is weary. His understanding is unsearchable. 29 He gives power to the weak, And to those who have no might He increases strength. 30 Even the youths shall faint and be weary, And the young men shall utterly fall, 31 But those who wait on the Lord shall renew their strength; They shall mount up with wings like eagles, They shall run and not be weary, They shall walk and not faint.

Isaiah 41:10

Fear not, for I am with you; Be not dismayed, for I am your God. I will strengthen you, Yes, I will help you, I will uphold you with My righteous right hand.'

Jeremiah 17:7

Blessed is the man who trusts in the Lord, And whose hope is the Lord.

Habakkuk 3:17-19

Though the fig tree may not blossom, Nor fruit be on the vines; Though the labor of the olive may fail, And the fields yield no food; Though the flock may be cut off from the fold, And there be no herd in the stalls—18 Yet I will rejoice in the Lord, I will joy in the God of my salvation. 19 The Lord God is my strength; He will make my feet like deer's feet, And He will make me walk on my high hills.

John 14:1-3

Let not your heart be troubled; you believe in God, believe also in Me. 2 In My Father's house are many mansions; if it were not so, I would have told you. I go to prepare a place for you. 3 And if I go and prepare a place for you, I will come again and receive you to Myself; that where I am, there you may be also.

Romans 8:37

Yet in all these things we are more than conquerors through Him who loved us.

Romans 12:12 ESV

Rejoice in hope, be patient in tribulation, be constant in prayer.

Romans 15:13 ESV

May the God of hope fill you with all joy and peace in believing, so that by the power of the Holy Spirit you may abound in hope.

I Corinthians 10:13 ᴇsᴠ

No temptation has overtaken you that is not common to man. God is faithful, and he will not let you be tempted beyond your ability, but with the temptation he will also provide the way of escape, that you may be able to endure it.

I Corinthians 15:55-57

"O Death, where is your sting? O Hades, where is your victory?" 56 The sting of death is sin, and the strength of sin is the law. 57 But thanks be to God, who gives us the victory through our Lord Jesus Christ.

II Corinthians 4:6-10

For it is the God who commanded light to shine out of darkness, who has shone in our hearts to give the light of the knowledge of the glory of God in the face of Jesus Christ. 7 But we have this treasure in earthen vessels, that the excellence of the power may be of God and not of us. 8 We are hard pressed on every side, yet not crushed; we are perplexed, but not in despair; 9 persecuted, but not forsaken; struck down, but not destroyed—10 always carrying about in the body the dying of the Lord Jesus, that the life of Jesus also may be manifested in our body.

II Corinthians 12:9-10

And He said to me, "My grace is sufficient for you, for My strength is made perfect in weakness." Therefore most gladly I will rather boast in my infirmities, that the power of Christ may rest upon me. 10...For when I am weak, then I am strong.

I Peter 1:3-8

Blessed be the God and Father of our Lord Jesus Christ, who according to His abundant mercy has begotten us again to a living hope through the resurrection of Jesus Christ from the dead, 4 to an inheritance incorruptible and undefiled and that does not fade away, reserved in heaven for you, 5 who are kept by the power of God through faith for salvation ready to be revealed in the last time. 6 In this you greatly rejoice, though now for a little while, if need be, you have been grieved by various trials, 7 that the genuineness of your faith, being much more precious than gold that perishes, though it is tested by fire, may be found to praise, honor, and glory at the revelation of Jesus Christ, 8 whom having not seen you love. Though now you do not see Him, yet believing, you rejoice with joy inexpressible and full of glory,

I Peter 1:18-19

Knowing that you were not redeemed with corruptible things, like silver or gold, from your aimless conduct received by tradition from your fathers, 19 but with the precious blood of Christ, as of a lamb without blemish and without spot.

I Peter 5:7 ESV

Casting all your anxieties on him, because he cares for you.

Ways to Remember Your Child

1. Give a monetary donation to your local church or another reputable charity.

2. Plant a tree, rose bush, or other type of shrubbery on the actual due date or a significant birthday (as in a first or fifth birthday).

3. Do a photo session with your infant. There are professionals willing to donate their time at the loss of a child (www.nowilaymedowntosleep.org).

4. Pick out a piece of jewelry to have special meaning just to you.

5. Make a scrapbook of the cards and notes received at your time of loss.

6. Annually donate a floral arrangement to your church, a nursing home, or even the maternity ward's nurses' station.

7. Financially "adopt" an overseas child from a reputable missionary agency.

8. Organize a support group in your community to minister to others.

9. Post your story on a bereavement website.

10. Donate baby Bibles to your local hospital as gifts for new parents.

Symptoms of Denial

Webster defines denial as "a psychological defense mechanism in which confrontation with a personal problem or with reality is avoided by denying the existence of the problem or reality."

A mother may be in denial over her child's death if she is regularly displaying any of the following:

1. Avoids discussing the death

2. Continues on as if nothing has happened

3. Refuses to help with funeral arrangements

4. Continues to prepare for the baby

5. Withdraws from those closest to her

6. Continues to wear maternity clothes after a loss

7. Refuses to believe and accept the truth

Things to Consider at Your Time of Loss

1. Will you have a funeral, a memorial service, a small family service, or nothing at all?

2. Will you choose a name?

3. Will you donate any of your child's organs if someone approaches you about doing so?

4. Will you take pictures of your baby and with your baby?

5. Will you allow others to see your baby?

6. Will you bathe and dress your baby?

Prayers to God

Trying to Accept

Dear God,

I feel so confused and hurt right now. What was supposed to be one of the happiest times in my life has turned into the greatest disappointment and sadness that I have ever felt. I am overwhelmed with emotions that are hard to put into words or thoughts. Suddenly, anger seems to have full reign; yet I know that is wrong. Even with people surrounding me, I feel so alone. My loneliness triggers despair and hopelessness. I want to understand your plan for me and my child, and yet these and other emotions hold me back from knowing what to say or how to best convey my feeling to you at this time. Because you are the God who created me and knows me even better than I know myself, please help me through this very difficult time. I am crying out to you right now. Please give peace and comfort, and please help me to accept that what you have brought about is the best thing at this time.

Amen.

Accepting Yet Still Hurting

Dear God,

Your ways certainly are not my ways, and your plans are not my plans. Even though my heart is broken and my world seems so upside down right now, I submit to your plan for my life and my baby's life. I had dreams that have turned into a nightmare, dreams I will never see come true; but I am giving those dreams to you. I still find it hard to overcome many of the emotions that want to choke out any hint of happiness that could find its way back into my life. Please give hope and healing to my hurting heart.

Amen.

Still Trying to Go On After Six or More Months

Dear God,

Nothing has ever been so hard for me to move past in my life. Others need me, but I still cry at the smallest remembrance of my wee one. I know he is in your presence, but my heart aches to have him here. Feelings of guilt often overcome me when I find myself laughing or enjoying something. I know my joy is not wrong, but it seems so out of place without my child. In your patient mercy, please give me joy and laughter again, without guilt. Help me turn my weak will over to you and accept completely the decision you made for me.

Amen.

Acceptance

Dear God,

I still miss my child. At times I long to hold, smell, touch, even just see her small face. However, in your tender kindness, you have brought me to a place of complete acceptance of the fact that she is now with you and that I will one day see her in Heaven. I praise you for your faithfulness and mercies that you daily renew. Thank you for being my stronghold during my time of trial. Your grace has been sufficient and will continue to sustain me. May your will continue to be done in my life, and please help me to see the good that you promised will come from all of this.

Amen.

Helping Your Wife

The loss of a baby has been the cause of divorce in many homes. Of course, this is a very stressful time and can become a crisis point in even the strongest of marriages. However, the loss of a child can also be a time when a husband and wife are drawn together as they grieve and seek the Lord during their time of loss. This list is included especially for husbands to have a starting point of ideas of how to help and comfort your wife right now.

1. Love her and demonstrate your love.

2. Pray with her, for her, and for your relationship.

3. Read the Bible together.

4. Touch her a lot.

5. Hold her often.

6. Let her see and know your emotions.

7. Check on her emotions regularly—even weeks and months later.

8. Give her time to be alone.

9. Give her time to talk.

10. Give her time to cry.

11. Give her time to heal physically.

12. Take care of your other children for her as much as is possible.

13. Take on additional household duties.

14. Assure her of your belief in God's sovereign choices for your family.

15. In no way directly cast blame at her, or even hint at casting blame, for the loss of your baby.

What Not to Say to a Grieving Mom

Not all of you reading this book have gone through a recent loss. Some of you are just seeking advice to know better how to help a friend or loved one go through such a trial. This list of what not to say to a grieving mom is included for you.

1. You can always have more children.

2. Be happy you already have a child.

3. It just wasn't meant to be.

4. Call me if you need anything. (The grieving mom won't call.)

5. God must have a reason for allowing this.

6. The sooner you find closure the better.

7. If this happened to me, I think I would just die.

8. It's probably time to move on.

9. Be glad you weren't further along in your pregnancy.

10. This too shall pass.

11. Your baby is much better off.

12. This is very common.

13. It's probably easier for you this way since you didn't have time to get "attached."

14. If you would have just done this or wouldn't have done that…

15. Everything will be back to normal soon.

Letters I Wrote to the First Baby I Lost

September 27, 1992

Dear Little Person,

Two days ago we found out you may never be an actual part of our lives. You've already become an important, unforgettable part; however, we may never get to meet.

The doctors think your little heart may have stopped beating four weeks ago. This is very difficult to understand and accept at this time since you are still safely tucked inside me. The feelings of guilt can be overwhelming at times thinking I did something to cause your little heart to quit. But, I know that God has you in His care and whatever happens is in His plans for you and me. He tells me in Isaiah 55:8: "For My thoughts are not your thoughts, Nor are your ways My ways."

Thinking about never seeing you, never holding you, never nursing you makes my heart break, yet I know that if these things do take place, then someday in Heaven we will get to meet for the first time. The song "God Makes No Mistakes" keeps coming to mind; and although the lyrics are hard to think through, I know that they are true—God doesn't make mistakes.

If we find out the doctors have misdiagnosed our problem, then it will be a very happy day, and I will once again get to imagine what you will look like, what your sister will think about you, and how proud your daddy will look when you are born. We will know that God has something very special in the future for you. If we learn that the doctors are right, then I want you to know we still love you very much. You will always have a special place in our hearts.

May God's will be done in both of our lives.

Lovingly,
Your Mommy

October 14, 1992

My Dear Little Child,

It has taken me a week and a half to be able to write this. I guess I felt like this would be a final good-bye and then I would have to forget you. However, that will not be the case. Yes, this is for me to say good-bye, but I certainly will never forget you. Time, I know, will help heal the ache I have whenever I think of you; but time will never erase the fact that for a few short months you were a special little part of me.

On October 2, the Lord saw fit to take you from me. The week following was a week of emotions like

I've never experienced before—emotions like guilt, emptiness, despair, frustration, dread, heartbreak. However, I've been able to work through all these different feelings and realize that there was nothing I did or did not do that caused your death.

I still wonder what you would have been—a girl or a boy—who you would have looked like, what color hair you would have had; but I cannot dwell on it because I know that all these things were not meant for me to know right now. The Lord wanted you in Heaven, and I will see you there someday.

You will always be remembered and loved as a part of our family.

Until we meet in Heaven ~

Lovingly,
Your Mommy

For You are my hope, O Lord God; You are my trust from my youth. 6 By You I have been upheld from birth; You are He who took me out of my mother's womb. My praise shall be continually of You.

Psalm 71:5-6

My Journal of Hope

*I*t is now up to you to choose to embark on your journey of healing, as you apply the things you have learned about hope in this book. At this moment, you may not be ready to begin writing your thoughts and prayers, but claim a verse of comfort and promise and write that down in the space provided. God says in his Word in Isaiah 57:18-19, "I have seen his ways, and will heal him; I will also lead him, And restore comforts to him And to his mourners. '… Peace, peace to him who is far off and to him who is near,' Says the Lord, 'And I will heal him.'" After you have claimed several verses and have written them down, I would encourage you, over time, to begin writing your own journal of hope, using the headings as a guide for your thoughts. In the months and years to come, you will have a place to revisit where you can remember what God taught you and how he gave hope and healing to your wounded heart.

My Verses of Hope

_____

_____

_____

_____

_____

_____

_____

_____

_____

_____

_____

_____

_____

_____

_____

_____

_____

_____

_____

_____

My Story of Loss

_____

_____

_____

_____

_____

_____

_____

_____

_____

_____

_____

_____

_____

_____

_____

_____

_____

_____

_____

_____

_____

_____

My Thoughts Right Now

A Letter to My Baby

_____

_____

_____

_____

_____

_____

_____

_____

_____

_____

_____

_____

_____

_____

_____

_____

_____

_____

_____

_____

_____

_____

My Prayer to God

_____

_____

_____

_____

_____

_____

_____

_____

_____

_____

_____

_____

_____

_____

_____

_____

_____

_____

_____

_____

_____

Endnotes

1   Used with permission. Matt Slick, "God's Sovereignty," accessed on April 14, 2010, http://www.carm.org/christianity/devotions/gods-sovereignty.

2   Elisabeth Kübler-Ross, On Death and Dying (Abingdon, Oxon: Routledge, 2009), First published 1970 by Tavistock Publications Limited.

3   Charles Haddon Spurgeon, Beside Still Waters. Compiled and edited by Roy H. Clarke. (Nashville, TN: Thomas Nelson, Inc., 1999), p. 29.